BUSY BEES
SPRING

Fun for Two's and Three's

By Elizabeth McKinnon and Gayle Bittinger
Illustrated by Barb Tourtillotte

Totline® Publications
A Division of Frank Schaffer Publications, Inc.
Torrance, California

We wish to thank the following teachers, childcare workers, and parents for contributing some of the ideas in this book: Deborah Balmer, Mesa, AZ; Ellen Bedford, Bridgeport, CT; Janice Bodenstedt, Jackson, MI; Patty Claycomb, Ventura, CA; Frank Dally, Ankeny, IA; Maureen Gutyan, Williams Lake, B.C.; Judy Hall, Wytheville, VA; Lindsay Hall, Wytheville, VA; Gemma Hall-Hart, Bellingham, WA; Mary Haynes, Lansing, MI; Nancy Heimark, Alamogordo, NM; Colraine Pettipaw Hunley, Doylestown, PA; Julie Israel, Ypsilanti, MI; Barbara Jackson, Denton, TX; Neoma Kreuter, El Dorado Springs, MO; Kathy McCullough, Everett, WA; Margo Miller, Westerville, OH; Susan Moon, Allentown, PA; Micki Nadort, Coquitlam, B.C.; Sharon Olson, Minot, ND; Susan M. Paprocki, Northbrook, IL; Lois E. Putnam, Pilot Mountain, NC; Beverly Qualheim,Marquette, MI; Polly Reedy, Elmhurst, IL; Betty Silkunas, Lansdale, PA; Carla C. Skjong, Tyler, MN; Diane Thom, Maple Valley, WA; Elizabeth Vollrath, Stevens Pt., WI; Kristine Wagoner, Puyallup, WA; Angela Wolfe, Miamisburg, OH; Bonnie Woodard, Shreveport, LA; Maryann Zucker, Reno, NV.

Editorial Staff:

Editorial Manager: Kathleen Cubley
Editors: Susan Hodges, Jean Warren
Copy Editor: Kris Fulsaas
Proofreader: Mae Rhodes
Editorial Assistants: Kate Ffolliott, Erica West

Design and Production Staff:

Art Managers: Uma Kukathas, Jill Lustig
Book Design: Lynne Faulk
Layout Production: Sarah Ness
Cover Design: Brenda Mann Harrison
Cover Illustration: Barb Tourtillotte
Busy Bee Drawings: Susan Dahlman
Production Manager: Jo Anna Brock

ISBN 1-57029-026-1

Library of Congress Catalog Number 94-61016
Printed in the United States of America
Published by Totline Publications

Editorial Office: P.O. Box 2250
Everett, WA 98203

Business Office: 23740 Hawthorne Blvd.
Torrance, CA 90505

20 19 18 17 16 15 14 13 12 11 10 9 8 7 6 5

INTRODUCTION

Welcome to the Spring edition of *Busy Bees—Fun for Two's and Three's,* an idea resource for teachers and parents of children 2 through 3 years old.

Busy Bees—Fun for Two's and Three's offers age-appropriate, fun, attention-getting activities. It is filled with hands-on projects and movement games that are just right for busy little ones. Also included are language and snack suggestions suitable for two's and three's, plus a rhyme and one or more songs to accompany each chapter.

The ideas in this book are designed to complement your everyday curriculum. The chapters are listed in an order that you may wish to follow day by day, although each one stands alone and can be used in a pick-and-choose fashion. You will find that the activities are perfect for those times when you want to interject group participation and purposefulness into your usual free-play agenda.

We hope that the suggestions in *Busy Bees—Fun for Two's and Three's* will act as a catalyst and inspire you to add ideas and activities of your own to those in the book.

Happy teaching!

CONTENTS

May

MARCH

Rainbows

HANDS-ON SCIENCE

Exploring Rainbows

Make a rainbow in your room for your children to discover. Place a small mirror in a glass of water and tilt it against the side of the glass. Then stand the glass in direct sunlight so that the mirror reflects a rainbow on a wall. Can your children identify any of the rainbow colors (red, orange, yellow, green, blue, purple)?

Variation: Create several rainbows by hanging crystal prisms in direct sunlight.

MOVEMENT

Rainbow Play

Draw a large rainbow on butcher paper and tape it to the floor. Let your children take turns walking, crawling, and tiptoeing along the rainbow arcs. Then let them try hopping or jumping over the rainbow.

RHYME

A Rainbow Gay

From big gray clouds
The raindrops fell,
Drip, drip, drip,
One day.
  (Flutter fingers downward.)
Until the sunlight
Changed them all
Into a
Rainbow gay.
  (Form arc above head with arms.)

Adapted Traditional

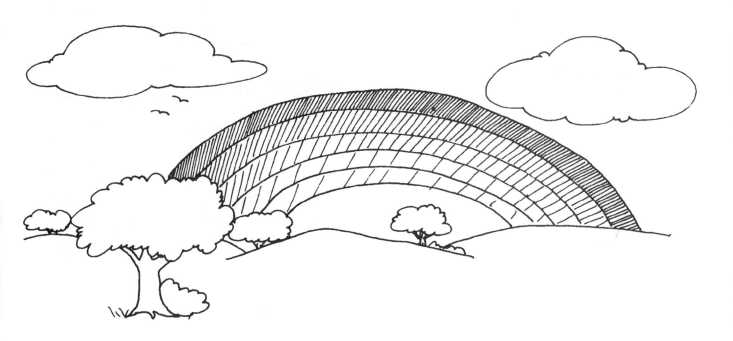

SONG

Rainbow Colors

Sung to: "Hush, Little Baby"

Rainbow purple,
Rainbow blue.
Rainbow green,
And yellow, too.
Rainbow orange,
Rainbow red.
Rainbow smiling
Overhead.

Come and count the
Colors with me.
How many colors
Can you see?
One, two, three,
Up to green.
Four, five, six
Colors can be seen.

Jean Warren

LANGUAGE IDEA

Display a picture of a rainbow
and name each of the colors with
your children.

SNACK IDEA

Serve each of your children
a "rainbow" of fruit in a clear-
plastic cup.

Birds

HANDS-ON ART

Feathery Birds

Set out feathers (available at craft stores). Give each of your children a large bird shape cut from construction paper. Have the children brush glue on their shapes. Then let them place the feathers on top of the glue to make Feathery Birds.

MOVEMENT

Bird Moves

Have your children pretend to be birds. Play music and let them "fly" around the room, flapping their wings as they go. Occasionally, have them stop flying and hop around, looking for pretend food to eat.

RHYME

Once I Saw a Little Bird

Once I saw
A little bird
Go hop,
Hop, hop.
And I called,
"Little bird,
Will you stop,
Stop, stop?"

I was opening
The window
To say,
"How do you do."
But he shook
His little tail,
And far away
He flew.

Adapted Traditional

SONG

Little Bird, Little Bird

Sung to: "Twinkle, Twinkle, Little Star"

Little bird, little bird,
Fly around,
Up to the sky,
Down to the ground.
Little bird, little bird,
Flap your wings.
Open your beak
And sweetly sing.
Little bird, little bird,
Fly to your nest.
Now it is time
To take a rest.

Susan M. Paprocki

LANGUAGE IDEA

Make bird sounds by whistling or chirping. Ask your children to listen carefully and try to imitate the sounds.

SNACK IDEA

When snacktime is over, let your children help gather up the crumbs and scatter them around outside for the birds to eat.

Hats

Hat Play

In a box, place various kinds of hats such as a rain hat, a baseball cap, a firefighter hat, a bathing cap, a felt derby, a straw hat, and a sunbonnet. Set out the hat box and several mirrors. Let your children play with the hats, trying them on and looking at themselves in the mirrors. Encourage the children to act out different characters as they try on the hats.

MOVEMENT

Musical Hats

Collect one hat for each of your children and arrange them in a large circle on the floor. Play music and have the children hop, skip, or dance around the hats. When you stop the music, let each child pick up a hat and put it on. Then have the children put the hats back on the floor in a circle and start the game again.

RHYME

Caps for Sale

Caps for sale,
Caps for sale.
Caps upon
My head.
  (Touch head.)
Caps for sale,
Caps for sale.
Yellow, blue,
And red.

Jean Warren

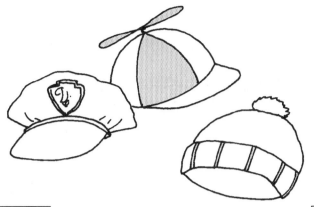

SONGS

Hats on People

Sung to: "Frere Jacques"

Hats on people,
Hats on people,
Every day,
Every day.
Hats for working,
Hats for working.
Hats for play,
Hats for play.

Jean Warren

Hats, Hats, Hats

Sung to: "Three Blind Mice"

Hats, hats, hats.
Hats, hats, hats.
I love hats.
I love hats.
Hats to wear
For work or play.
Hats for night
And hats for day.
Hats from here
And far away.
I love hats.

Jean Warren

LANGUAGE IDEA

Set out your hat box from the activity Hat Play (page 12). Ask your children to find a red hat, a hat they would wear when swimming, a hat a firefighter uses, etc.

SNACK IDEA

Make cone-shaped hats for your children to decorate and wear at snacktime.

Wind

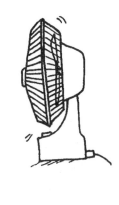

HANDS-ON SCIENCE

Exploring Wind

Collect objects that are heavy, such as a wood block, a metal spoon, and a stone, and objects that are light such as a feather, a cotton ball, and a piece of yarn. Turn an electric fan on low to create "wind." Let your children experiment with placing the different objects in the path of the "wind." Which objects blow away? Which ones don't? (Note: Activities that involve the use of electrical appliances require adult supervision at all times.)

Variation: Do the activity outdoors on a windy day.

MOVEMENT

Blowing Winds

Tape crepe-paper streamers to your children's arms. Have the children move around the room, pretending to be the wind. Encourage them to dip, sway, and twirl around as they "blow."

RHYME

Wind Tricks

The wind is full of
Tricks today.
It blew our
Newspaper away.
It chased the trash can
Down the street,
And almost blew us
Off our feet!

Adapted Traditional

I See the Wind

Sung to: "Hush, Little Baby"

I see the wind
When the leaves
Dance by.
I see the wind
When the clothes
Wave "Hi!"
I see the wind
When the trees
Bend low.
I see the wind
When the flags
All blow.

I see the wind
When the kites
Fly high.
I see the wind
When the clouds
Float by.
I see the wind
When it blows
My hair.
I see the wind
Most everywhere.

Jean Warren

LANGUAGE IDEA

Tell your children a story about the wind. Let them accompany the story by making whooshing sounds.

SNACK IDEA

At snacktime, let your children choose foods to eat that would not blow away in the wind.

Kites

HANDS-ON ART

Paper-Bag Kites

Give each of your children a paper lunch bag to decorate with crayons. Punch two holes near the top of each bag and tie on string handles. Then take your children outside and let them run with their Paper-Bag Kites to make them "fly" in the wind.

RHYME

Come Fly a Kite

Come fly a kite
And watch it sail
(Hold hand high.)
Across the sky,
Waving its tail!
(Wave hand back and forth.)

Author Unknown

MOVEMENT

Kites in the Sky

Have your children stand in an open area. Play music and let them pretend to be kites flying in the sky. Encourage them to swoop up and down, twirl around, and wiggle their "tails" as they fly.

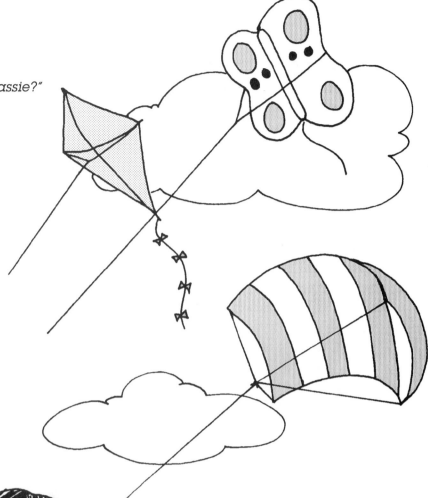

SONG

Kite Flying

Sung to: "Did You Ever See a Lassie?"

Oh, can you see
The kite fly,
The kite fly,
The kite fly?
Oh, can you see
The kite fly
Way up in the sky?
The wind blows it
This way,
And then blows it
That way.
Oh, can you see
The kite fly
Way up in the sky?

Janice Bodenstedt

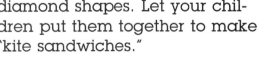

LANGUAGE IDEA

Talk with your children about things that fly such as kites, birds, airplanes, and insects.

SNACK IDEA

Cut bread and cheese slices into diamond shapes. Let your children put them together to make "kite sandwiches."

Diamonds

Sparkling Diamonds

Let your children make Sparkling Diamonds. For each child, cut two diamond shapes out of clear self-stick paper. Remove the backing from one shape and help the child sprinkle glitter or metallic confetti on the sticky side. Remove the backing from the second shape and place it sticky-side down on top of the first shape. To display the diamonds in a window, punch a hole in the top of each shape and tie on ribbon hangers.

MOVEMENT

Diamond Walk

Arrange a long piece of yarn in a diamond shape on a carpet. Let your children take turns walking, tiptoeing, hopping, or crawling around the edges of the diamond.

RHYME

A Diamond

This is a diamond,
As you can see.
  (Point to a diamond shape.)
Now draw one
In the air with me.
  (Draw diamond with finger.)

Neoma Kreuter

SONG

Diamonds on the Floor

Sung to: "The Farmer in the Dell"

The diamonds
Are on the floor.
The diamonds
Are on the floor.
Pick one up
And say its name,
And then pick up
One more.

Place construction paper diamond
shapes on the floor. Repeat the song
until all the shapes have been
picked up.

Lindsay Hall

LANGUAGE IDEA

Show your children pictures of
diamond-shaped traffic signs and
discuss what the signs mean.

SNACK IDEA

Serve your children crackers
shaped like triangles. Let them
arrange the crackers in pairs to
form diamond shapes on their
plates.

Houses

Dollhouse Play

Use cardboard boxes to make
dollhouses for your children.
Cover the inside walls with
wallpaper samples and attach
self-stick paper "vinyl" to the
floors. Add simple dollhouse
furniture made from small boxes,
thread spools, and wood blocks.
Let your children play with toy
people in the dollhouses.

MOVEMENT

Cleaning House

Ask your children to imagine that
they are house cleaners. Lead
them in pretend activities such as
dusting tables and chairs, washing and polishing windows, and
sweeping and scrubbing floors.
Encourage the children to use lots
of "elbow grease" as they work.

RHYME

Two Little Houses

Two little houses
Closed up tight.
  (Close fists.)
Let's open the windows
And let in some light.
  (Open fists.)

Adapted Traditional

SONG

Build a House

Sung to: "Row, Row, Row Your Boat"

Build, build,
Build a house.
Build it
Tall and wide.
Make some
Windows.
Make a
Door.
Then walk
Right inside!

Elizabeth McKinnon

LANGUAGE IDEA

Talk with your children about the different rooms in a house and what they are used for.

SNACK IDEA

Cut pieces of construction paper into simple house shapes to make placemats for the snack table.

The Three Little Pigs

HANDS-ON DRAMATIC PLAY

Building Houses

Set out a child-size wheelbarrow filled with various sizes of blocks. Let your children wheel it to a "building site" in the room. Then let them work together to construct one or more block houses.

MOVEMENT

Blowing Down Houses

Have your children stand in an open area, pretending to be houses made of straw and sticks. Move among them, huffing and puffing. Have the "houses" fall to the floor as you "blow them down." Continue by letting the children take turns huffing and puffing.

RHYME

The Little Pigs' Houses

The Three Little Pigs
To town did go.
They built three houses
All in a row.

The first was made of straw.
The second was made of sticks.
And the third was made
With some big, red bricks.

Elizabeth McKinnon

SONG

Who Built a House?

Sung to: "Mary Had a Little Lamb"

Who built a house
That was made of straw,
Made of straw,
Made of straw?
Who built a house
That was made of straw?
The first Little Pig,
That's who.

Who built a house
That was made of sticks,
Made of sticks,
Made of sticks?
Who built a house
That was made of sticks?
The second Little Pig,
That's who.

Who built a house
That was made of bricks,
Made of bricks,
Made of bricks?
Who built a house
That was made of bricks?
The third Little Pig,
That's who.

Elizabeth McKinnon

LANGUAGE IDEA

Read or tell a simplified version of "The Three Little Pigs."

SNACK IDEA

Let your children help spread peanut butter on graham cracker rectangles. Then stack the rectangles, one on top of the other, to make "brick wall" snacks.

Bubbles

Making Bubbles

Use the recipe below to make a bubble mixture. Give each of your children a plastic straw with a hole punched near the top to use as a bubble blower. Or let them dip small plastic coat hangers or plastic lids with the centers removed into the bubble mixture and wave them in the air to make bubbles.

Bubble Mixture

2 cups Joy dishwashing detergent
6 cups water
¾ cup Karo light corn syrup

Mix ingredients together, shake well, and let the mixture sit for a few hours. (Note: Watch to see that the area where bubbles pop does not become too slippery.)

Floating Bubbles

Let your children pretend to float around the room like bubbles. Have them clap and drop to the ground when they "pop."

Blowing Bubbles

Blowing bubbles
Every day,
I blow them
All around.
  (Blow.)
Then I watch them
Float up high,
Or pop
Upon the ground.
  (Clap once.)

Jean Warren

SONGS

I'm a Little Bubble

Sung to: "I'm a Little Teapot"

I'm a little bubble,
Soft and light.
I float high up
Like a kite.
See me float down lower.
Watch me stop.
Then I'll surprise you
With a pop!

Diane Thom

Blow, Blow

Sung to: "Row, Row, Row Your Boat"

Blow, blow,
Blow, blow, blow.
I blow,
And then I stop.
For if I keep on
Blowing,
My bubble's sure
To pop!

Jean Warren

LANGUAGE IDEA

Sit with your children in a circle.
Blow bubbles into the middle of
the circle and ask the children to
describe them.

SNACK IDEA

Serve sparkling apple juice or
grape juice in clear-plastic cups.
Have your children observe the
bubbles.

Straws

HANDS-ON ART

Straw Necklaces

Give each of your children a piece of colored telephone wire with a small loop twisted at one end. Cut plastic straws into short segments. Help the children string the straw segments onto their wire pieces. When they have finished, twist the ends of each child's wire piece together to make a necklace for slipping over his or her head.

MOVEMENT

Flexible Straws

Let your children pretend to be Flexible Straws. Have them stand straight with arms at their sides. Then have them try bending up and down from the waist, first to the left, then to the right, then backward and forward.

RHYME

Sipping Our Juice

Our glasses of juice
Are all in a row.
We put in our straws
Just like so.
We take some big sips,
And what do you think?
Our juice disappears
As quick as a wink!

Adapted Traditional

My Sipping Straw

Sung to: "The Muffin Man"

Watch me use
My sipping straw,
My sipping straw,
My sipping straw.
Watch me use
My sipping straw
To sip and sip and sip.

I use my straw
To sip my juice,
Sip my juice,
Sip my juice.
I use my straw
To sip my juice.
I sip and sip and sip.

Repeat, substituting *milk* for *juice*.

Elizabeth McKinnon

LANGUAGE IDEA

Ask your children to name different things that they can drink with straws.

SNACK IDEA

Serve juice or milk in plastic glasses and give your children straws to use for sipping.

Green

HANDS-ON ART

Painting With Evergreens

Cut evergreen branches into sprigs to use as paintbrushes. Pour green tempera paint into containers and set out a sheet of light green or white construction paper for each child. Let your children dip the evergreen sprigs into the paint and brush them on their papers to create green designs.

MOVEMENT

Green Animal Moves

Have your children get down on all fours. Play some fast music and let them scamper around the floor like little green lizards. Then play some slow music and have them crawl around like big green turtles.

RHYME

Green

Green, we love you.

Yes, we do!

Grass and trees

And lettuce, too!

Repeat, substituting the names of other green things for *grass*, *trees*, and *lettuce*.

Jean Warren

SONG

What Is Green?

Sung to: "Three Blind Mice"

Green, green, green.
Green, green, green.
What is green?
What is green?
The grass, the plants,
The trees, and the leaves,
The lettuce we put
In the salad we eat,
The grasshoppers hopping
Around our feet—
They all are green.

Diane Thom

LANGUAGE IDEA

Place a large piece of green paper on a table. Have your children find green objects, name them, and place them on top of the paper.

SNACK IDEA

Let your children snack on frozen green peas.

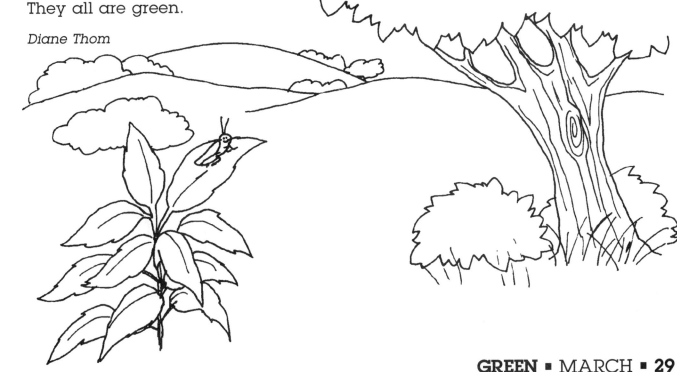

Green Foods

HANDS-ON COOKING

Making a Green Salad

Let your children help wash green lettuce leaves and pat them dry. Have them tear the leaves into pieces and place them in a large salad bowl. Then let them help you prepare other green foods to add to the salad bowl such as fresh spinach leaves, cucumber, zucchini, green onions, celery, green bell peppers, and sprouts. Top the salad with a favorite dressing.

MOVEMENT

Green Foods Game

For each of your children, attach one green construction-paper square to the floor. Have the children circle around the squares as you call out the names of different foods. Whenever you name a green food, have each child find a green square and sit down on it. Continue as long as interest lasts.

RHYME

Green Vegetables

Green vegetables
Are plants we eat.
They're so good.
What a treat!
   (Lick lips.)
Celery, beans,
And broccoli—
They help us grow
So healthily.
   (Rub tummy and smile.)

Gayle Bittinger

SONG

Green Fruits

Sung to: "Twinkle, Twinkle, Little Star"

One green melon,
Extra nice.
Pretty please,
Give me a slice!
Two green apples,
Really sweet.
What a super-duper
Treat!
Three green grapes,
So great to munch.
Let's have some
Today for lunch!

Lois E. Putnam

LANGUAGE IDEA

Make a picture chart of green foods. Display the chart and name the foods with your children.

SNACK IDEA

Let your children enjoy their salad from the activity Making a Green Salad (page 30).

Shamrocks

HANDS-ON ART

Paper-Plate Shamrocks

Give each of your children three small paper plates. Let the children use brushes or sponge pieces to paint their plates green. Help them sprinkle on green glitter while the paint is still wet. When the paint has dried, staple each child's plates together and attach a green construction-paper stem to make a shamrock.

MOVEMENT

Shamrock Search

Cut shamrock shapes out of green felt and place them around the room. Let your children search for the shamrocks as you sing the song "Looking for Shamrocks" (page 33). Whenever the children find a shamrock, have them place it on a flannelboard and take a bow.

RHYME

My Shamrock

I have a little
Shamrock.
It's green
As green can be.
Watch me as I
Count the leaves.
One, two,
Three.

Elizabeth McKinnon

SONGS

I Wish I Were a Shamrock

Sung to: "Did You Ever See a Lassie?"

Oh, I wish
I were a shamrock,
A shamrock, a shamrock.
Oh, I wish
I were a shamrock
For St. Patrick's Day.
With leaves
One, two, three
As green
As can be.
Oh, I wish
I were a shamrock
For St. Patrick's Day.

Elizabeth McKinnon

Looking for Shamrocks

Sung to: "The Farmer in the Dell"

Let's look for
Shamrocks now.
Let's look for
Shamrocks now.
And when we find
A bright green one,
Then we can
Take a bow!

Place shamrock shapes around the room for your children to discover as you sing.

Jean Warren

LANGUAGE IDEA

Display a full-page picture from a magazine. Let your children add shamrock stickers to the picture as you give directions such as these: "Place a shamrock on the tree. Place a shamrock next to the dog. Place a shamrock under the wagon."

SNACK IDEA

Cut sandwiches into shamrock shapes using a shamrock-shaped cookie cutter.

Dancing

Finger-Paint Fun

Give each of your children a piece of butcher paper with a spoonful of finger paint in the center. Play a recording of ballet music (or similar music) and let your children "dance" their fingers and hands across their papers as they finger-paint designs.

MOVEMENT

Dance, Dance, Dance

Play different kinds of fast and slow music and let your children dance to it. Encourage them to bend, sway, tap, and twirl as they dance around the room.

RHYME

Magic Feet

Have you seen
My magic feet,
Dancing down
The magic street?
Sometimes fast,
Sometimes slow,
Sometimes high,
Sometimes low?

Jean Warren

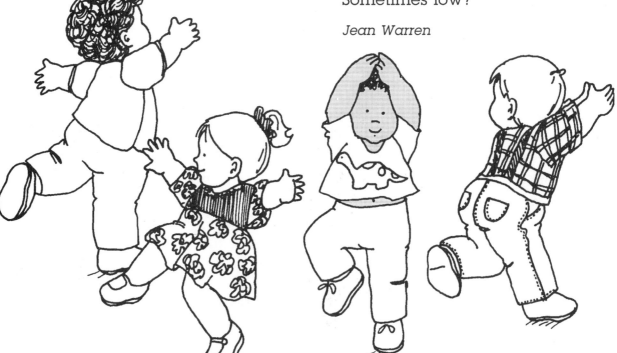

Here We Go Dancing

Sung to: "The Mulberry Bush"

Here we go dancing
Round the room,
Round the room,
Round the room.
Here we go dancing
Round the room,
So early
In the morning.

Repeat, each time substituting a different phrase, such as *past the chairs* or *out the door,* for *round the room.*

Elizabeth McKinnon

Dance, Dance

Sung to: "Skip to My Lou"

Dance, dance,
Just like me.
Dance, dance,
Just like me.
Dance, dance,
Just like me.
Dance, little Cody,
Just like me.

Sing the song for each of your children, substituting the name of the child for *Cody.*

Jean Warren

LANGUAGE IDEA

With your children, talk about and demonstrate different dance words such as *tap, twirl, slide,* and *dip.*

SNACK IDEA

Let your children dance in a line to the snack table.

Frogs

HANDS-ON SCIENCE

Discovery Table

On a table, arrange various kinds of frog items for your children to discover and play with. Include things such as pictures of frogs, plastic frogs, toy frogs that can be made to swim in a tub of water, and a tape recording of frog sounds. Encourage the children to talk about the frog items as they play.

MOVEMENT

Jumping Frogs

Show your children how to jump like frogs. Have them crouch down and place their hands out in front of them on the floor. Then have them jump forward, raising their arms high in the air before returning to a crouching position. Encourage the children to take both big and little frog jumps as they move around the room.

RHYME

A Little Frog

A little frog
In a pond am I.
Hippity, hoppity, hop.
   (Hop fist up and down.)
Watch me jump
In the air so high.
Hippity...hoppity...hop!
   (Hop fist as high as possible.)

Adapted Traditional

In the Pond

Sung to: "The Farmer in the Dell"

The frog lives
In the pond.
The frog lives
In the pond.
It reaches high
To catch a fly.
The frog lives
In the pond.

Jean Warren

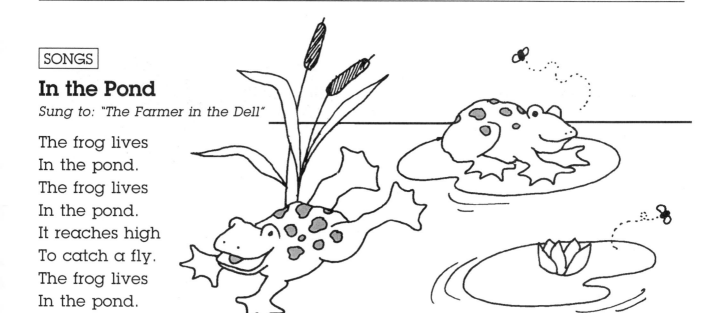

Did You Ever See a Frog?

Sung to: "Did You Ever See a Lassie?"

Did you ever
See a frog,
A frog, a frog?
Did you ever
See a frog
Jump this way
And that?
Jump this way
And that way.
Jump this way
And that way.
Did you ever
See a frog
Jump this way
And that?

Adapted Traditional

LANGUAGE IDEA

Read or tell a frog story. Whenever your children hear the word *frog*, have them say "ribbit."

SNACK IDEA

Let your children hop like little frogs to the snack table.

Lambs

HANDS-ON ART

Woolly Lambs

Give each of your children a large lamb shape cut from white construction paper. Set out cotton balls and shallow containers of glue. Let your children dip the cotton balls into the glue and then place them all over their lamb shapes to make Woolly Lambs.

MOVEMENT

Frolicking Lambs

Have your children pretend to be lambs while you act as their parent. Let them frolic and leap about until you call out "Time to sleep!" When you signal that it's time to wake up, have the "lambs" start frolicking again.

RHYME

Little Lamb

This little lamb
Eats grass.
　　(Point to thumb.)
This little lamb
Likes to play.
　　(Point to index finger.)
This little lamb
Drinks water.
　　(Point to middle finger.)
This little lamb
Runs away.
　　(Point to ring finger.)
And this little lamb
Does nothing at all
　　(Point to little finger.)
But wag its tail
All day.
　　(Wiggle little finger.)

Adapted Traditional

Baby Sheep

Sung to: "Mary Had a Little Lamb"

Lambs are little
Baby sheep,
Baby sheep,
Baby sheep.
Lambs are little
Baby sheep,
And they say
"Baa, baa."

Lambs are soft
And woolly, too,
Woolly, too,
Woolly, too.
Lambs are soft
And woolly, too.
The wool makes
Clothes for you.

Carla C. Skjong

LANGUAGE IDEA

Cut a lamb shape out of white posterboard. Cover the shape with cotton and attach it to a craft stick to make a puppet for telling lamb stories.

SNACK IDEA

Serve your children a snack that lambs would like to eat such as apple slices topped with alfalfa-sprout "grass."

Mary Had a Little Lamb

Mary's Lamb

Cut a lamb shape out of three different colors of posterboard. Out of the same three posterboard colors, cut a child shape to represent Mary. Attach pieces of magnetic strip to the backs of the shapes. Place the "Mary" shapes on a magnet board. Let your children take turns placing the matching-colored lamb shapes next to the Mary shapes.

MOVEMENT

Following Mary

Let each of your children have a turn pretending to be Mary. Have the other children pretend to be lambs and line up behind her. Let "Mary" walk all around the room while the lambs follow along behind her, imitating her movements as they go.

RHYME

Mary Had a Little Lamb

Mary had a
Little lamb.
Its fleece was
White as snow.
And everywhere
That Mary went,
The lamb was
Sure to go.

Traditional

Little Lambs

Sung to: "Mary Had a Little Lamb"

Little lambs
Are leaping high,
Leaping high,
Leaping high.
Little lambs
Are leaping high.
Little, little,
Lambs.

Bonnie Woodard

LANGUAGE IDEA

Ask your children to name places
where Mary's little lamb might
go with her.

SNACK IDEA

Use a cookie cutter to make
lamb-shaped cookies. Let your
children help spread on white
frosting.

Baa, Baa, Black Sheep

Black Sheep

Cut black yarn into short pieces.
Pour glue into shallow containers
and set out brushes. Give each of
your children a lamb shape cut
from white construction paper.
Let the children brush glue on
their shapes and place the yarn
pieces on top of the glue to make
Black Sheep.

MOVEMENT

Three Bags Full

Set out three large garbage bags.
Let your children crumple sheets
of newspaper and stuff them into
the bags until the bags are com-
pletely full.

RHYME

Baa, Baa, Black Sheep

Baa, baa, black sheep,
Have you any wool?
Yes, sir, yes, sir,
Three bags full.
One for my master,
And one for my dame,
And one for the little boy
Who lives down the lane.

Traditional

SONG

I Love Sheep
Sung to: "Three Blind Mice"

I love sheep,
I love sheep.
I count them
In my sleep.
They jump all night
Over fences high.
They jump so high
They reach the sky.
They help me sleep,
And that is why
I love sheep.

Jean Warren

LANGUAGE IDEA

Display and talk about items that are made of wool such as yarn, sweaters, socks, and mittens.

SNACK IDEA

Serve each of your children a snack in a paper bag.

Cotton

Counting Cotton Balls

Let each of your children fill a small container, such as a toothpaste box, a yogurt cup, or a plastic sandwich bag, with cotton balls. As each child empties his or her container, count the number of cotton balls together with the group.

MOVEMENT

Cotton-Ball Toss

Place one or two large containers on the floor and have your children stand several feet away from them. Let the children take turns tossing cotton balls into the containers.

RHYME

Cotton

I love cotton
Very much.
Soft to feel,
Soft to touch.

Adapted Traditional

LANGUAGE IDEA

Ask your children to name things that are "soft as cotton."

SNACK IDEA

Serve each of your children a piece of fruit topped with a spoonful of whipped-topping "cotton."

SONG

Blow, Blow

Sung to: "Row, Row, Row Your Boat"

Blow, blow
The cotton balls.
Blow them
Just like so.
Blow them hard,
Blow them soft.
Move them fast
And slow.

Elizabeth McKinnon

Hard and Soft

Hard or Soft?

In a box, place several items that are hard such as a stone, a spoon, and a block. Add several items that are soft such as a cotton ball, a woolen sock, and a piece of foam rubber. Let your children take turns removing items from the box and sorting them into two groups: items that are hard and items that are soft.

MOVEMENT

Obstacle Course

Set up a hard and soft Obstacle Course for your children to follow. Have them do activities such as sliding down a hard slide, jumping into soft pillows, hopping across a hard floor, and rolling over a soft mattress.

RHYME

Soft as a Pillow

Soft as a pillow.
Soft as a sock.
Hard as a hammer.
Hard as a rock.

Elizabeth McKinnon

Hard and Soft Song

Sung to: "London Bridge"

Touch the rock.
It feels so hard,
Feels so hard,
Feels so hard.
Touch the rock.
It feels so hard.
Hard, hard rock.

Touch the fur.
It feels so soft,
Feels so soft,
Feels so soft.
Touch the fur.
It feels so soft.
Soft, soft fur.

Repeat, substituting the names of other hard and soft things for *rock* and *fur*.

Elizabeth McKinnon

LANGUAGE IDEA

Place hard and soft objects in a bag. As your children remove them, incorporate the objects into a story that you make up.

SNACK IDEA

Serve foods that have hard and soft textures such as pretzels with whipped cream cheese or apple slices with yogurt.

Bunnies

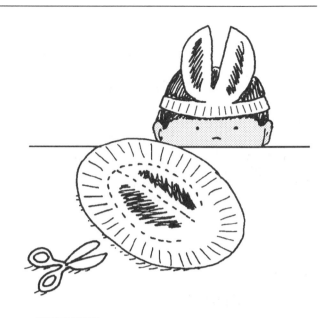

HANDS-ON ART

Bunny Ears

Let your children help make Bunny Ears to wear. Give them each a paper plate and let them color on the center parts with pink crayons. Then cut each plate along the dotted lines as shown in the illustration. Fold up the pink "ears" before slipping the plates over the children's heads.

MOVEMENT

Bunny Hop

Help your children put on their "ears" from the activity Bunny Ears (this page). Then play music and let the children hop around the room like bunnies.

RHYME

Little Bunny

Here's a
Little bunny
With ears so
White and long.
  (Hold up two fingers.)
Watch it hop
And hop about
On legs
So small and strong.
  (Hop hand around.)

Author Unknown

SONG

I'm a Little Bunny

Sung to: "I'm a Little Teapot"

I'm a little bunny.
Watch me hop.
   (Hop.)
Here are my two ears.
See how they flop.
   (Flop hands at sides of head.)
Here's my cotton tail,
And here's my nose.
   (Wiggle hips, then nose.)
I'm all furry
From my head to my toes.
   (Point to head, then feet.)

Susan M. Paprocki

LANGUAGE IDEA

Bring in a live bunny or a stuffed toy bunny for your children to pet and describe.

SNACK IDEA

Serve your children fresh vegetables such as carrot sticks or lettuce leaves. Encourage them to nibble like bunnies as they eat.

Rabbit, Rabbit, Carrot Eater

Carrot Mural

Cut thin, flat sponges into carrot shapes. Set out a piece of butcher paper or a large piece of construction paper. Let your children dip the sponge pieces into orange tempera paint and press them on the paper to make carrot prints. Use felt-tip markers to draw on green carrot tops. Then add a construction-paper rabbit to complete the mural.

RHYME

Rabbit, Rabbit, Carrot Eater

Rabbit, rabbit,
Carrot eater.
He says there is
Nothing sweeter
Than a carrot
Every day.
Munch and crunch
And run away!

Traditional

MOVEMENT

Carrot Munch

Let your children pretend to be rabbits. Have them hop around as you name different foods. Whenever you call out "Carrots!" have the "rabbits" stop hopping and pretend to nibble and munch. Continue as long as interest lasts.

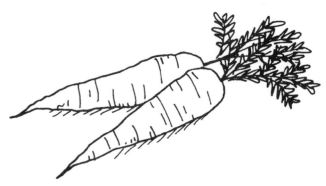

I'm a Little Rabbit

Sung to: "I'm a Little Teapot"

I'm a little rabbit
Soft and white.
> *(Point to self.)*

Here are my ears
> *(Hold up two fingers behind head.)*

And my tail so white.
> *(Hold fist behind back.)*

I like to nibble carrots
Every day.
> *(Pretend to eat carrot.)*

And then I hop
And hop away.
> *(Hop.)*

Judy Hall

LANGUAGE IDEA

Recite "Rabbit, Rabbit, Carrot Eater" (page 52), each time letting your children substitute a different word for *carrot*.

SNACK IDEA

Make a sweet carrot snack by soaking carrot sticks in pineapple juice for one or more hours.

Carrots

HANDS-ON DRAMATIC PLAY

Pulling up Carrots

Purchase carrots with green, leafy tops. Plant the carrots in a big tub of dirt so that they look as if they are actually growing. Let your children pull up the carrots and prepare them for eating by breaking off the tops and scrubbing them clean.

MOVEMENT

Giant Carrot Pull

Ask your children to help you pull up a pretend giant carrot that is growing in the ground. Let them grab on behind you in a line and pull as you direct them. When the "carrot" pops out of the ground, have everyone tumble backward onto the floor.

RHYME

Plant a Carrot Seed

Plant a little
Carrot seed.
Water it
Just so.
Soon a carrot,
Orange and green
Will start to
Grow and grow!

Elizabeth McKinnon

Carrots in a Row

Sung to: "Down by the Station"

Out in
My garden
Early in
The morning,
See my
Little carrots
All in
A row.
See all
My friends
Come to help
Me pull them.
Pull, pull,
Pull, pull.
Watch us go!

Jean Warren

Grow, Little Carrots

Sung to: "Row, Row, Row Your Boat"

Grow, grow,
Little carrots,
Growing in
A row.
I will take
Good care of you.
I'll water you
Just so.

Have your children walk back and
forth as they sing, pretending to water
carrots.

Jean Warren

Ask your children to tell you their
favorite ways to eat carrots such
as cut into sticks, cut into rounds
and cooked, or stir-fried with
other vegetables.

Cut the carrots from the activity
Pulling Up Carrots (page 54) into
sticks. Serve them plain or with
a dip.

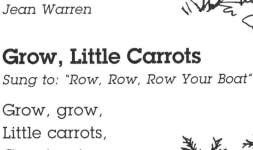

Crayons

HANDS-ON ART

Drawing With Crayons

Give each of your children a piece of white construction paper. Set out crayons in different sizes and colors, and let the children experiment with drawing designs. Include crayons with the paper wrappers removed so that the children can color with the sides as well as the ends.

MOVEMENT

Crayons in a Box

Have your children stand together, straight and tall, pretending to be crayons in a box. When you pretend to open the box, have the "crayons" tumble out and roll all over the floor.

RHYME

Pretty Color Crayons

Pretty color
Crayons—
Red, green,
And blue,
Orange, purple,
And yellow.
I love them,
Yes, I do!

Jean Warren

Color Crayons

Sung to: "Mary Had a Little Lamb"

Rachel has
A red crayon,
Red crayon,
Red crayon.
Rachel has
A red crayon.
She can draw
An apple.

Daniel has
A green crayon,
Green crayon,
Green crayon.
Daniel has
A green crayon.
He can draw
A leaf.

Continue with similar verses about each
of your children.

Jean Warren

LANGUAGE IDEA

Display a box of crayons and
name each of the colors with
your children.

SNACK IDEA

Place a butcher paper "table-
cloth" on the snack table. Let
your children decorate it with
crayons while they wait for their
snack to be served.

Purple

HANDS-ON ART

Purple Finger Paint

For each of your children, fill a resealable plastic sandwich bag about one-third full with shaving cream. Add drops of red and blue food coloring and reseal the bags. Have the children squeeze their bags and watch as the shaving cream turns purple. Then let them finger-paint with the shaving cream on pieces of white paper.

RHYME

I Met a Purple Cow

I met a purple cow
Walking down the street.
She had purple eyes.
She had purple feet.
She looked just like
The other cows do—
Except she was purple
And her milk was, too!

Jean Warren

MOVEMENT

Purple Parade

Attach purple crepe-paper streamers to cardboard-tube "handles." Give the tubes to your children and let them parade around the room as you play music. As the children march, call out directions such as "Raise your purple streamers high!" or "Twirl your purple streamers around!"

Purple Is Dancing

Sung to: "When Johnny Comes Marching Home"

Purple is dancing
All around,
Hurray, hurray.
Purple is dancing
All around.
We hope it stays.
Grapes and plums
And violets, too.
Purple, we love you,
Yes, we do!
And we're all
So glad that
Purple is here today!

Give your children pictures of purple grapes, plums, and violets to hold as they sing and dance.

Jean Warren

LANGUAGE IDEA

Make up a story about a world in which everything is purple. As you tell the story, illustrate it with a purple crayon.

SNACK IDEA

Mix milk with grape juice and pour it into clear-plastic cups to make "purple cows."

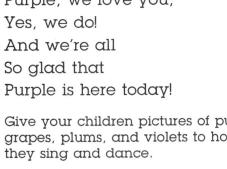

Humpty Dumpty

Putting Humpty Together

For each of your children, cut an egg shape out of white poster-board and decorate it to make a "Humpty Dumpty." Cut each shape into two puzzle pieces. Let your children play with their puzzles, "breaking" Humpty in two, then putting him back together.

MOVEMENT

Tip and Fall

Let your children sit on the floor. Have them tip over and "fall" as you recite the rhyme below.

Humpty Dumpty
Sitting on a wall.
Humpty Dumpty
Tip and fall.

Adapted Traditional

RHYME

Humpty Dumpty

Humpty Dumpty
Sat on a wall.
Humpty Dumpty
Had a great fall.
All the king's horses
And all the king's men
Couldn't put Humpty
Together again.

Traditional

See Him Fall

Sung to: "Frere Jacques"

Humpty Dumpty,
Humpty Dumpty,
Sitting on a wall,
Sitting on a wall.
Now he takes
A tumble.
Now he takes
A tumble.
See him fall,
See him fall.

Elizabeth McKinnon

LANGUAGE IDEA

Talk with your children about things that break and things that don't break when they fall.

SNACK IDEA

Give your children hard-cooked eggs to break open and eat. Talk about why Humpty's shell could not be put back together again.

Eggs

Texture Eggs

Cut eight or more egg shapes out of cardboard. Divide the shapes into pairs. Cover each pair with a different textured material such as corduroy, burlap, flocked wallpaper, or felt. Place the eggs in a basket for your children to touch and match.

MOVEMENT

Egg Roll

Have your children lie on the floor, pretending to be eggs. Then play music and let them roll all around. Remind them not to bump into one another or they might "break!"

RHYME

Little Egg

Once there was
A little egg
That jumped down
To the floor.
It started
Rolling all around,
Then rolled
Right out the door!

Jean Warren

SONG

Eggs, Eggs, Eggs

Sung to: "Twinkle, Twinkle, Little Star"

Eggs in buckets,
Eggs in bins.
Eggs in baskets,
Eggs in tins.
Eggs in green grass,
Eggs in clover.
Eggs, eggs, eggs,
Yes, eggs all over.
Eggs for children
Just like me.
Eggs for springtime fun,
Yippee!

Lois E. Putnam

LANGUAGE IDEA

Over separate bowls, crack open a raw egg and a hard-cooked egg. Ask your children to tell how the eggs are alike and how they are different.

SNACK IDEA

Let your children help make deviled eggs to eat at snacktime.

Colored Eggs

Egg Play

Place 12 plastic eggs in a basket. Set out the basket and an empty egg carton. Let your children take turns putting the eggs into the cups of the egg carton and then emptying them back into the basket. Talk about the egg colors as the children play.

MOVEMENT

Egg Hunt

Hide colored plastic eggs around the room and give each of your children a small basket. Let the children search for the eggs and place the ones they find in their baskets. When all the eggs have been found, hide them again.

RHYME

Eggs in My Basket

I've eggs in
My basket.
Oh, yes, dear,
I do.
I've eggs in
My basket,
And here's one
For you!

I've green eggs
And pink ones
And purples
And blues.
I've eggs in
My basket.
Now which
Will you choose?

Lois E. Putnam

Colored Eggs

Sung to: "Jingle Bells"

Colored eggs,
Colored eggs,
Eggs of red
And blue.
Here are lots of
Colored eggs,
All for me
And you.
Yellow eggs,
Purple eggs,
Eggs of orange
And green.
Aren't these the
Most beautiful eggs
That you have
Ever seen?

Maureen Gutyan

Hunting for Eggs

Sung to: "The Mulberry Bush"

Here we go hunting
All around,
All around,
All around.
Here we go hunting
All around
To find
Our colored eggs.

Additional verses: Here we go hopping
all around; Here we go tiptoeing all
around; Here we go crawling all around.

Micki Nadort

LANGUAGE IDEA

Hide a small object inside a colored plastic egg. Make up a story about the object and reveal what it is by opening the egg at the end of the story.

SNACK IDEA

Serve each of your children a small wrapped snack placed inside a colored plastic egg.

Scrambled Eggs

HANDS-ON COOKING

Making Scrambled Eggs

Place a mixing bowl on a low table. Help each of your children crack an egg into the bowl and stir it with a fork. Add a tablespoon of water or milk for each egg and let the children take turns stirring the mixture until it is well blended. If desired, have them add small pieces of ham or cheese. Cook the eggs in a small amount of butter or margarine over medium heat until they are set.

MOVEMENT

Roll and Scramble

Have your children pretend to be eggs. As you call out "Roll, roll, roll!" have them roll around on the floor. Whenever you call out "Scramble!" have them stop rolling, lie flat, then wiggle their arms, legs, and bodies all around.

RHYME

A Special Treat

At breakfast time,
For a special treat,
I like scrambled
Eggs to eat.

Elizabeth McKinnon

SONG

Scrambling Eggs

Sung to: "Old MacDonald Had a Farm"

Scrambling eggs
In the frying pan.
Scrambling them
Around.
Scrambling eggs
As fast as we can.
Scrambling round
And round.
With a scramble,
Scramble here,
And a scramble,
Scramble there.
Here a scramble,
There a scramble,
Everywhere a
Scramble, scramble.
Scrambling eggs
In the frying pan.
Scrambling them around.

Elizabeth McKinnon

LANGUAGE IDEA

After doing the activity Making Scrambled Eggs (page 66), make a set of picture cards showing the steps you followed. Let your children arrange the cards in the proper order.

SNACK IDEA

Let your children enjoy their homemade scrambled eggs from the activity Making Scrambled Eggs (page 66) with toast or muffins.

Chicks

Fuzzy Chicks

Give each of your children a chick shape cut out of yellow construction paper. Tear yellow cotton balls into small pieces. Let your children brush glue on their chick shapes. Then have them place the yellow cotton pieces on top of the glue.

Variation: Use yellow feathers instead of cotton.

MOVEMENT

Hatching Chicks

Have your children crouch down near the floor, pretending to be chicks inside eggs. Have them peck at their pretend shells until the shells break open. Then let the newly hatched "chicks" scamper around the room, cheeping and flapping their wings.

RHYME

Little Chick

Snuggled
Down inside
An egg
That was white,
Was a tiny
Little chick
With its head
Tucked in tight.

Then it
Tilted its head,
Tapped the egg
With its beak,
And quickly
Popped out.
Cheep, cheep,
Cheep!

Colraine Pettipaw Hunley

SONG

Little Chicks

Sung to: "Ten Little Indians"

Hear the little chicks
Cheeping in the barnyard.
Hear the little chicks
Cheeping in the barnyard.
Hear the little chicks
Cheeping in the barnyard.
Cheep, cheep, cheep,
Cheep, cheep.

See the little chicks
Pecking in the barnyard.
See the little chicks
Pecking in the barnyard.
See the little chicks
Pecking in the barnyard.
Peck, peck, peck,
Peck, peck.

Elizabeth McKinnon

LANGUAGE IDEA

Read or tell a story about chicks. Whenever your children hear the word *chick*, have them make cheeping sounds.

SNACK IDEA

Let your children decorate construction-paper placemats with chick stickers. Or give them yellow paper chick shapes to glue on the mats.

Weaving

Weaving Fun

Tie a large net, such as a badminton net, between two chairs. Place weaving materials, such as fabric strips, yarn pieces, and strips of paper, in separate containers. Let your children choose materials and poke or weave them through the holes in the net any way they wish.

MOVEMENT

Follow the Leader

Place chairs in a wide circle. Have your children line up behind you. Then have them follow as you weave in and out of the circle between the chairs. Sing "Weave In and Out the Chairs" (page 71) as you go.

RHYME

Over and Under

Over and under
And in and out,
Weaving my yarn
I go.
Under and over
And out and in.
I weave my yarn
Just so.

Elizabeth McKinnon

SONG

Weave In and Out the Chairs

Sung to: "Go In and Out the Window"

Weave in and out
The chairs.
Weave in and out
The chairs.
Weave in and out
The chairs.
As we have done before.

Repeat, each time substituting a
different word, such as *blocks*, *books*,
or *toys*, for *chairs*.

Adapted Traditional

LANGUAGE IDEA

Talk about the words *over*, *under*,
in, and *out* and have your children demonstrate what each
one means.

SNACK IDEA

Serve the day's snack on woven
placemats.

Baskets

Basket Play

Set out large and small baskets. Also set out large and small blocks, toys, or other objects. Let your children experiment with putting the large objects into the large baskets and the small objects into the small baskets.

MOVEMENT

Basket Parade

Give your children baskets with handles. Let them fill their baskets with plastic eggs or small plastic toys. Then play music and let the children carry their baskets around the room in a "parade."

RHYME

My Basket

A little egg,
Where does it hide?
Deep in my basket—
Just peek inside!

Repeat, each time substituting a different word, such as *crayon*, *block*, or *toy*, for *egg*.

Elizabeth McKinnon

SONG

In Your Basket

Sung to: "Ten Little Indians"

Find a block and
Put it in your basket.
Find a block and
Put it in your basket.
Find a block and
Put it in your basket.
Put it in
Your basket now.

Repeat, each time substituting a different word, such as *crayon*, *toy*, or *egg*, for *block*.

Jean Warren

LANGUAGE IDEA

Place objects in a basket and start telling a story. Incorporate the objects into the story as your children remove them from the basket.

SNACK IDEA

Wrap snack foods in waxed paper or aluminum foil and serve them to your children in a basket.

Full and Empty

Fill Them, Empty Them

Let your children place blocks, toys, or crumpled newspaper into boxes or bags until the containers are full. Then have them remove the objects to make the containers empty. Continue by having the children fill and empty cups of sand or water.

MOVEMENT

All Together Now

Set out an empty plastic wading pool. Let your children all squeeze into the pool until it is full of bodies. Then have them step out to make the pool empty again.

Variation: Use a large shallow box instead of a wading pool.

RHYME

My Cup

My cup is empty.
I'll pour in some tea.
    (Pretend to pour.)
Now it is full,
As you can see.
    (Hold out pretend cup.)

Elizabeth McKinnon

Fill the Bag

Sung to: "Row, Row, Row Your Boat"

Fill, fill,
Fill the bag.
Fill it now
With me.
First it's empty,
Then it's full.
Full as full
Can be.

Repeat, each time substituting a different word, such as *box*, *cup*, or *plate*, for *bag*.

Elizabeth McKinnon

LANGUAGE IDEA

With your children, recite the rhyme "Baa, Baa, Black Sheep" (page 42).

SNACK IDEA

As your children eat their snack, talk about cups, plates, or bowls that are full and empty.

FULL AND EMPTY ▪ APRIL ▪ **75**

Grass

Planting Grass Seeds

Let your children help spoon potting soil into several small paper cups. Have them sprinkle grass seeds on top of the soil. Show them how to press the seeds down a bit before adding small amounts of water. Then have the children place the cups in a sunny spot, add water regularly, and watch for the seeds to sprout.

MOVEMENT

Playing in the Grass

Take your children outdoors to a yard or a park and let them roll and play in the grass. If desired, let them take off their shoes and run through the grass barefoot.

RHYME

In the Grass

Watch the
Little bunnies
Peeking through
The grass.
   (Peek through fingers.)
When they
See me,
They duck
Down fast!
   (Crouch down to floor.)

Polly Reedy

SONG

See Us Playing

Sung to: "Did You Ever See a Lassie?"

See us playing
In the green grass,
The green grass,
The green grass.
See us playing
In the green grass
That grows in
Our yard.
We jump and we run.
We have so much fun.
See us playing
In the green grass
That grows in
Our yard.

Elizabeth McKinnon

LANGUAGE IDEA

Sit on the grass with your children while you read or tell them a story.

SNACK IDEA

Let your children have a picnic outdoors on the grass.

Chalk

HANDS-ON ART

Drawing With Chalk

Give your children pieces of colored chalk. Let them try drawing with the chalk on different surfaces such as a chalkboard or a slate, pieces of construction paper, cardboard squares, or an outdoor sidewalk.

MOVEMENT

Eraser Fun

Have your children pretend to be giant chalkboard erasers. Ask them to imagine that someone has drawn all over the floor or a wall with chalk. Then let them use their bodies to "erase" the drawings.

RHYME

Our Colored Chalk

Let's go
Outdoors,
Find a
Long sidewalk,
And draw
Designs
With our
Colored chalk.

Elizabeth McKinnon

Drawing Pictures

Sung to: "Clementine"

Drawing pictures,
Drawing pictures,
Drawing pictures
With my chalk.
Drawing pictures
On the sidewalk,
Drawing pictures
With my chalk.

Drawing apples,
Drawing apples,
Drawing apples
With my chalk.
Drawing apples
On the sidewalk,
Drawing apples
With my chalk.

Continue with similar verses
about other kinds of pictures.

Elizabeth McKinnon

LANGUAGE IDEA

Tell your children a story and
illustrate it by drawing simple
chalk pictures.

SNACK IDEA

Let your children decorate pieces
of construction paper with chalk
designs to make placemats for the
snack table. Cover the mats with
clear self-stick paper, if desired.

Clouds

Sky Pictures

Give each of your children a piece of light blue construction paper. Stretch out cotton balls so that they resemble clouds. Let your children brush glue on their papers and arrange the cotton-ball "clouds" on top of the glue to make Sky Pictures.

MOVEMENT

Floating Clouds

Have your children stand in an open area, pretending to be clouds. Walk among the children, pretending to be the wind. As you gently touch the "clouds," have them float and drift across the pretend sky.

RHYME

Clouds in the Sky

Clouds in the sky,
All fluffy and white.
They hide the sun
That shines so bright.
    (Pretend to float like a cloud.)
They float about
The sky so blue,
And form so many
Great shapes, too.
    (Stretch body into different shapes.)

Angela Wolfe

Clouds

Sung to: "Twinkle, Twinkle, Little Star"

When I look
Into the sky,
I can see
The clouds go by.
They don't ever
Make a sound,
As the winds
Push them around.
Some go fast
And some go slow.
I wonder where
The clouds all go.

Frank Dally

LANGUAGE IDEA

Read your children a storybook
about clouds such as *It Looks Like
Spilled Milk.*

SNACK IDEA

Serve your children fruit or
pudding topped with whipped-
cream "clouds."

Rain

Rain Painting

On a rainy day, take your children outdoors. Give them each a paper plate on which you have sprinkled drops of food coloring. Let the children hold their plates in the rain for about a minute. When they bring their plates inside, talk about the designs created by the rain.

MOVEMENT

Rain Sounds

Let your children make light rainfall sounds by gently tapping their fingers and hands on a tabletop. Then have them make the sound of heavy rainfall by loudly tapping and stamping their feet on the floor.

RHYME

Pitter-Patter

Pitter-patter
Falls the rain
On the roof
And windowpane.
Softly, softly
It comes down,
Pitter-patter
All around.

Adapted Traditional

Rain Falling Down

Sung to: "Row, Row, Row Your Boat"

Rain, rain
Falling down,
Landing
All around.
What a lovely
Sound you make,
Splashing
On the ground!

Susan Moon

Sprinkle, Sprinkle

Sung to: "Twinkle, Twinkle, Little Star"

Sprinkle, sprinkle
On the ground.
Soft, wet rain is
Falling down.
Time for boots and
Coats and hats.
Open umbrellas
With a snap.
Sprinkle, sprinkle
On the ground.
Soft, wet rain is
Falling down.

Diane Thom

LANGUAGE IDEA

Teach your children the saying "April showers bring May flowers."

SNACK IDEA

Let your children dance like little raindrops to the snack table.

Umbrellas

Paper-Plate Umbrellas

Give each of your children a paper plate with a small hole poked in the middle. Let the children decorate the backs of their plates with crayons or felt-tip markers. When they have finished, have them stick their index fingers up through the holes in their plates to make "umbrellas."

MOVEMENT

Umbrella Moves

Have your children walk around like closed umbrellas with their arms straight down. Every now and then, tap out some rain sounds and have the "umbrellas" pretend to open up by raising their arms and holding them out at their sides. Whenever the rain sounds stop, have the children put their arms down again.

RHYME

It's Raining

It's raining,
It's raining,
Oh me, oh my!
    (Look upward.)
But our umbrellas
Will keep
Us dry!
    (Form umbrella above head with arms.)

Susan M. Paprocki

SONGS

Listen to the Raindrops

Sung to: "Ring Around the Rosie"

Walking 'neath umbrellas,
Listen to the raindrops.
Drip, drop, drip, drop.
They all fall down!

Lois E. Putnam

Rain on My Umbrella

Sung to: "Frere Jacques"

Drip, drip, drop, drop.
Drip, drip, drop, drop.
Drip, drip, drop.
Drip, drip, drop.
Rain on my umbrella,
Rain on my umbrella
Never stops.
Drip, drip, drop.

Betty Silkunas

LANGUAGE IDEA

Tell your children a story as you sit under a patio umbrella or an umbrella held in your hand.

SNACK IDEA

Wrap snack foods in aluminum foil or waxed paper and serve them from a child-size umbrella.

Boots

Find the Pairs

Collect pairs of different kinds of boots such as rain boots, snow boots, hiking boots, and cowboy boots. Mix up the boots and let your children take turns finding the pairs.

MOVEMENT

Boot Walk

Let your children take turns trying on the boots from the activity Find the Pairs (this page) and walking around in them. Or ask the children to walk around the room in pretend cowboy boots, pretend moon boots, pretend rain boots, etc.

RHYME

My Rain Boots

My rain boots
Are great to wear
To walk through puddles
Here and there,
To walk through puddles
On the ground
And splatter water
All around.

Lois E. Putnam

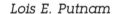

Our Boots

Sung to: "The Mulberry Bush"

This is the way
We pull on our boots,
    (Pretend to put on boots.)
Pull on our boots,
Pull on our boots.
This is the way
We pull on our boots
Before we go outside.

This is the way
We splash in our boots,
    (Walk in pretend boots.)
Splash in our boots,
Splash in our boots.
This is the way
We splash in our boots
That keep our feet so dry.

Elizabeth McKinnon

LANGUAGE IDEA

Slip a pair of boots on over your hands and have them "tell" a story about walking to different places.

SNACK IDEA

Let your children wear boots while they eat their snack.

Puddles

Exploring Puddles

Fill dishpans with sand and add enough water to each one to make a "puddle." Let your children play in the puddles with objects such as leaves, rocks, sponge pieces, and small plastic toys. Ask them to tell which items sink and which ones float.

Variation: Let your children play in rain puddles outdoors.

MOVEMENT

Puddle Jumping

Place carpet squares here and there on the floor. Ask your children to pretend that the squares are puddles. Let them practice jumping over the "puddles" or into them.

RHYME

Puddles

Puddles squish,
And puddles squash.
Puddles splish,
And puddles splosh.
Puddles shrink,
And puddles grow.
Puddles come,
And puddles go.

Lois E. Putnam

Rainy Day

Sung to: "Twinkle, Twinkle, Little Star"

Rainy, rainy,
Rainy day.
Water puddles
All for play.
The sky is cloudy,
But I don't mind.
Puddles, galoshes,
And mud pies.
Rainy, rainy,
Rainy day.
In the rain
I like to play.

Kristine Wagoner

Wading in Puddles

Sung to: "Did You Ever See a Lassie?"

Oh, it's fun to
Wade in puddles,
In puddles,
In puddles.
Oh, it's fun to
Wade in puddles
And splash
All around.
Splash this way
And that way.
Splash this way
And that way.
Oh, it's fun to
Wade in puddles
And splash
All around!

Elizabeth McKinnon

LANGUAGE IDEA

Ask your children to tell ways they can move their feet through puddles such as tiptoe, stomp, splash, or march.

SNACK IDEA

Make pudding and spoon it in "puddles" onto serving plates before chilling.

MAY

May Baskets

HANDS-ON ART

May Baskets

Give each of your children a large half-circle cut out of construction paper. Let the children decorate their papers with crayons or felt-tip markers. Roll each half-circle into a cone and secure the edges with tape. Complete the May Baskets by attaching pipe-cleaner handles and letting your children add real or paper flowers.

MOVEMENT

A May Basket for You

Have one of your children stand behind a door. Hang a May basket on the doorknob, knock on the door, then run and hide. Have the child open the door to find the basket. Then have the child hang the basket on the doorknob for another child. Continue until everyone has had a turn.

RHYME

A May Basket

Here's
A May basket.
Who can
It be for?
I know,
Let's hang it
On Christopher's
Door!

Recite the rhyme for each of your children.

Elizabeth McKinnon

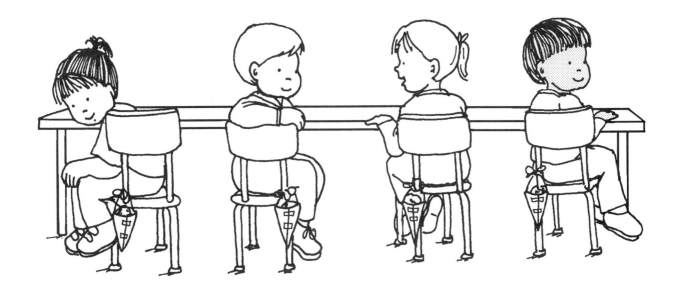

SONGS

May Basket

Sung to: "A-Tisket, A-Tasket"

A-tisket, a-tasket,
I made a May basket.
I filled it up
With flowers bright,
And hung it on
The door just right.

Jean Warren

I'm a Little Basket

Sung to: "I'm a Little Teapot"

I'm a little basket.
Look at me—
Filled full of flowers,
Pretty as can be.
Hang me on a friend's door
On May Day.
Then ring the bell
And run away.

Elizabeth McKinnon

LANGUAGE IDEA

Let your children add real or
paper flowers to a May basket
as you tell a story about it.

SNACK IDEA

At snacktime, hang a May basket
with a treat tucked inside on
each child's chair.

Flowers

Printed Flowers

Let your children finger-paint designs directly on a tabletop. When they have finished, place large flower shapes that have been cut from construction paper on top of the paint. Gently rub your hands over each shape. Then lift the shapes to reveal the printed designs.

MOVEMENT

Through the Flowers

Ask your children to pretend that they are standing in a flower garden. Then give directions such as these: "Tiptoe through the tulips. Dance through the daffodils. Roll through the roses. Crawl through the carnations. Hop through the heather."

RHYME

A Flower

My hand is a bud
Closed up tight,
Without a tiny
Speck of light.
　　(Close hand into fist.)
Then slowly the petals
Open for me,
And here is a beautiful
Flower, you see!
　　(Slowly open hand.)

Adapted Traditional

SONGS

Flowers Are Blooming

Sung to: "Mary Had a Little Lamb"

Flowers are blooming
Everywhere,
Everywhere, everywhere.
Flowers are blooming
Everywhere.
What a lovely day!

Flowers are blooming
Everywhere,
Everywhere, everywhere.
Flowers are blooming
Everywhere,
In the month of May.

Jean Warren

May Flowers

Sung to: "London Bridge"

Shout hurray for the
Flowers of May,
Flowers of May,
Flowers of May.
Shout hurray for the
Flowers of May.
Pretty springtime flowers!

Jean Warren

LANGUAGE IDEA

Make flower puppets by gluing pictures of flowers to the ends of craft sticks. Use the puppets for telling stories.

SNACK IDEA

Decorate a drinking straw for each of your children by attaching two flower stickers back to back near the top of the straw.

Mary, Mary, Quite Contrary

HANDS-ON ART

Garden Mural

Cut pictures of flowers out of magazines and seed catalogs. Set out a piece of butcher paper or a large piece of construction paper. Let your children brush glue on the paper. Then let them arrange the flower pictures on top of the glue to create a "flower garden."

MOVEMENT

Making a Garden

Ask your children to make an imaginary garden. Have them act out gardening activities such as pulling weeds, digging in the soil with pretend shovels and hoes, planting seeds, and watering.

RHYME

Mary, Mary, Quite Contrary

Mary, Mary,
Quite contrary,
How does your
Garden grow?
With silver bells
And cockleshells,
And pretty maids
All in a row.

Traditional

Mary Planted Her Garden

Sung to: "Mary Had a Little Lamb"

Mary planted her garden,
Her garden, her garden.
Mary planted her garden
With rows of pretty bells.

Mary planted her garden,
Her garden, her garden.
Mary planted her garden
With rows of cockleshells.

Let your children help make up
additional verses.

Gayle Bittinger

LANGUAGE IDEA

Make a "garden" of felt flowers
on a flannelboard. As you tell
a story about the flowers, let
your children take turns "pick-
ing" them.

SNACK IDEA

Cut different colors of construction paper into large flower
shapes to make placemats for
the snack table.

Scents

Scented Playdough

Make playdough, using a favorite recipe or the recipe below. Divide the dough into batches and add drops of a different food flavoring, such as peppermint, lemon, or vanilla, to each batch. Give your children the scented dough to play with.

Playdough Recipe

1 cup flour
½ cup salt
6 to 7 tablespoons water
1 tablespoon vegetable oil
Drops of food coloring (optional)

Mix together all of the ingredients. Store the playdough in the refrigerator in an airtight container.

MOVEMENT

Scented Dancing

Attach crepe-paper streamers to your children's wrists. Dab or spray a little cologne on the end of each streamer. Then play music and let your children wave their scented streamers as they dance around the room.

RHYME

A Little Nose

Katie has
A little nose.
It sniffs
And sniffs
Wherever
She goes!

Recite the rhyme for each of your children, substituting the child's name for Katie.

Elizabeth McKinnon

The Smelling Song

Sung to: "A-Tisket, A-Tasket"

I'm smelling,
I'm smelling.
My nose is
Busy smelling.
This is the song
I like to sing
When I smell
Most anything!

Kathy McCullough

Smells So Good

Sung to: "Frere Jacques"

Smells like springtime,
Smells like springtime.
Smells so good,
Smells so good!
I can smell the flowers.
I can smell the grass.
Smells so good,
Smells so good!

Continue with similar verses about
different times such as dinner time,
bath time, or holiday time.

Jean Warren

LANGUAGE IDEA

Talk about different kinds of
smells with your children.

SNACK IDEA

Use clean yogurt containers with
holes punched in their lids to
serve foods that have strong aro-
mas. Ask your children to sniff
and identify the foods before
eating.

Bees

Matching Bees

Cut six bee shapes out of yellow felt. Using a black felt-tip marker, decorate the first pair of bees with one stripe, the second pair with two stripes, and the third pair with three stripes. Add eyes and other details with the marker as desired. Place the bees on a flannelboard with a felt hive shape. Let your children take turns placing pairs of matching bees on the hive.

MOVEMENT

Buzzing Bees

Tape to the floor one construction-paper flower shape for each of your children. Have the children pretend to be bees. Play music and let them "buzz" around the room. Whenever you stop the music, have each "bee" find a flower to light on. Continue as long as interest lasts.

RHYME

The Beehive

Here is the beehive.
  (Make a fist.)
Where are the bees?
Hidden inside
Where nobody sees.
Here they come buzzing
Out of the hive.
  (Slowly open fist.)
One, two, three,
Four, and five!
  (Count fingers.)

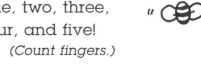

Adapted Traditional

Bumblebee, Bumblebee

Sung to: "Jingle Bells"

Bumblebee,
Bumblebee,
Landing on
My toes.
Bumblebee,
Bumblebee,
Now he's on
My nose.
On my arm,
On my leg,
Now on
My elbow.
Bumblebee,
Oh, bumblebee,
You land
And then you go!

Jean Warren

LANGUAGE IDEA

Make a bee out of construction paper and place tacky glue on the back. Let your children stick the bee around the room as you give directions such as these: "The bee is on the table. The bee is beside the door. The bee is under the chair."

SNACK IDEA

Serve toast, waffles, or fruit pieces topped with a taste of honey.

Dirt

Buried Treasure

Fill several dishpans with dirt and let your children watch as you bury "treasure" such as unusual rocks or small plastic toys. Set out plastic containers along with small shovels. Let the children dig in the dirt and shovel it into the containers as they search for the Buried Treasure.

MOVEMENT

Digging in the Dirt

Ask your children to imagine that they are gardeners standing in a big field of dirt. Have them bend over and pick up pretend shovels. Then give them directions for "digging" big holes, little holes, deep holes, and shallow holes in the pretend field.

RHYME

I Dig in the Dirt

I dig in the dirt
With my little spade.
Look at all
The holes I made!

Elizabeth McKinnon

SONG

I Love Dirt

Sung to: "Three Blind Mice"

I love dirt.
I love dirt.
Fun brown dirt,
Fun brown dirt.
I love to dig
Down in the ground.
I love to have
Dirt all around.
I love to pile
It in a mound.
I love dirt!

Gayle Bittinger

LANGUAGE IDEA

Place a cupful of dirt on a plate. Let your children take turns examining the dirt with a magnifying glass and telling what they see.

SNACK IDEA

Crumble chocolate wafers. Serve the dark brown crumbs sprinkled over vanilla yogurt.

Rocks

Rock Sorter

Make a Rock Sorter by cutting four or five holes from small to large in the lid of an empty shoe box. Give your children rocks of various sizes. Let them sort the rocks in the Rock Sorter by putting each rock through the hole that is closest to its size.

MOVEMENT

Rock Lifting

Have your children pretend to lift "rocks" of various sizes, place them in pretend buckets or wheelbarrows, and carry them across the room. End the activity by having the children work together to lift one "giant rock."

RHYME

A Little Rock

I went outside
And guess what I found—
A tiny little rock
Lying on the ground.

Repeat, substituting different words, such as *big* and *smooth*, for *tiny* and *little*.

Elizabeth McKinnon

Pick up the Rocks

Sung to: "Ten Little Indians"

Pick up the rocks.
Put 'em in your bucket.
Pick up the rocks.
Put 'em in your bucket.
Pick up the rocks.
Put 'em in your bucket.
Put 'em in your bucket now.

Dump all the rocks.
Dump 'em out your bucket.
Dump all the rocks.
Dump 'em out your bucket.
Dump all the rocks.
Dump 'em out your bucket.
Dump 'em out your bucket now.

Let your children pretend to pick up
rocks, put them into buckets, and dump
them out as you sing.

Jean Warren

LANGUAGE IDEA

Set out different sizes of rocks to
represent a family. Let your children make up stories about the
rock family members.

SNACK IDEA

Paint each of your children's
names on a separate rock. Place
the rocks on the snack table as
place cards.

Plants

Planting Seedlings

Bring in several plant seedlings (available at nurseries). Set out large flower pots, potting soil, and small spades. Let your children help fill the large pots with the soil, plant the seedlings in them, and add water. Place the pots in a sunny spot where the children can observe as the seedlings grow into plants.

MOVEMENT

Little Sprouts

Have your children crouch down near the floor, pretending to be seeds in the ground. As you pretend to add water, have the "seeds" sprout and gradually grow taller and taller until at last they become full-grown "plants."

RHYME

My Plants

I rake, and I hoe,
And I dig, dig, dig,
To plant my
Garden row.
The sun will shine,
And the rain will fall,
And my plants
Will grow and grow!

Margo S. Miller

Little Plants

Sung to: "Down by the Station"

Down in the garden,
Early in the morning,
  (Stand straight and tall.)
See the little plants
Bending to and fro.
  (Bend body back and forth.)
See the gentle breeze
Help them lift their arms.
  (Raise arms out at sides.)
Swish-swish, swish-swish,
Wave hello!
  (Wave arms gently up and down.)

Jean Warren

Show pictures of various kinds of plants, such as vegetables, trees, flowers, and grass, and have your children name them.

Decorate the snack table with different kinds of plants.

Caterpillars

Yarn Caterpillars

For each of your children, cut a large leaf shape out of green construction paper. Give each child a 4-inch piece of thick yarn for a "caterpillar." Let the children brush glue on their leaf shapes and arrange their Yarn Caterpillars on top of the glue.

MOVEMENT

Wiggling Caterpillars

Have your children stretch out on a carpet, pretending to be caterpillars on a leaf. As they crawl across the carpet, encourage the "caterpillars" to squirm and wiggle their bodies all around.

RHYME

Caterpillar

Caterpillar,
Creep.
Caterpillar,
Crawl.
Caterpillar,
Climb
All along
The wall.

Beverly Qualheim

Caterpillar, Caterpillar

Sung to: "Frere Jacques"

Caterpillar,
Caterpillar,
On the wall,
On the wall.
First you wiggle
This way.
Then you wiggle
That way.
Crawl, crawl, crawl.
Crawl, crawl, crawl.

Elizabeth McKinnon

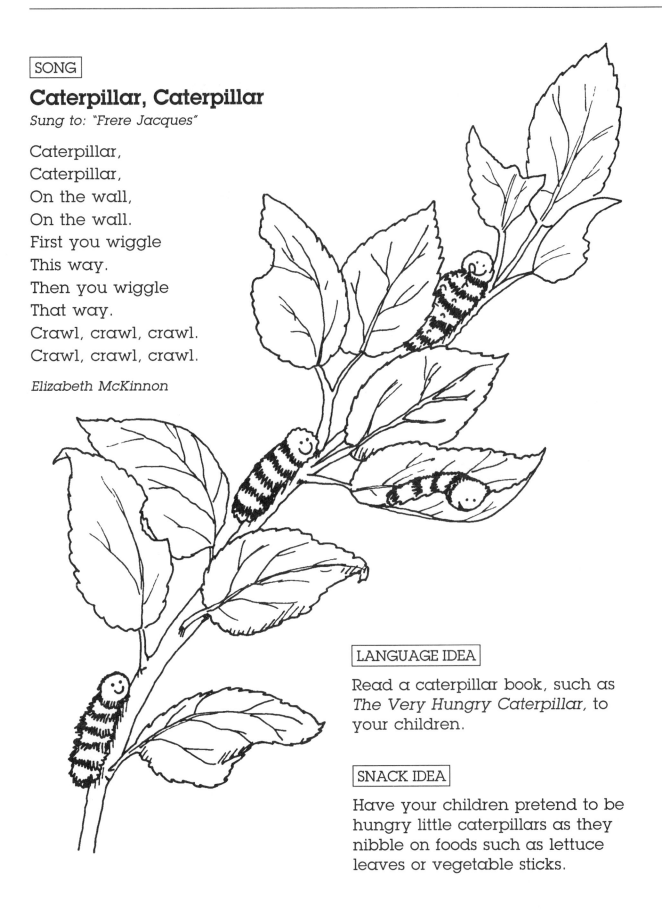

LANGUAGE IDEA

Read a caterpillar book, such as *The Very Hungry Caterpillar*, to your children.

SNACK IDEA

Have your children pretend to be hungry little caterpillars as they nibble on foods such as lettuce leaves or vegetable sticks.

Butterflies

Ink-Blot Butterflies

Let your children use eyedroppers to squeeze drops of paint onto pieces of light-colored construction paper. Help the children fold their papers in half. Have them press and smooth their papers, then unfold them to reveal the designs they have made. When the papers are dry, cut them into large butterfly shapes.

MOVEMENT

Butterfly Moves

Play music and let your children pretend to be butterflies flying around the room. Encourage them to gently wave their arms up and down as they pretend to float and flutter through the air.

RHYME

Flutter, Flutter

Flutter, flutter,
Butterfly.
Wave your wings
So you can fly.

Diane Thom

SONGS

Flutter By

Sung to: "Frere Jacques"

Flutter by,
Flutter by,
Butterfly,
Butterfly.
We love to
Watch you fly
In the clear
Blue sky.
Flutter by,
Butterfly.

Gayle Bittinger

Flutter, Flutter, Butterfly

Sung to: "Twinkle, Twinkle, Little Star"

Flutter, flutter,
Butterfly,
Floating in
The summer sky.
Floating by
For all to see,
Floating by
So merrily.
Flutter, flutter,
Butterfly,
Floating in
The summer sky.

Bonnie Woodard

LANGUAGE IDEA

Show your children a picture of a butterfly and help them name its different parts.

SNACK IDEA

Let your children attach butterfly stickers or cutouts to pieces of construction paper to make placemats for the snack table.

Brown

HANDS-ON ART

Scented Sandpaper

Give each of your children a square of brown sandpaper. Set out brown cinnamon sticks. Let the children use the cinnamon sticks like crayons to "color" on their sandpaper squares. Talk about the cinnamon color and scent as the children work.

MOVEMENT

Brown Bounce

For each of your children, tape a brown construction-paper square to the floor. Let the children bounce around like balls as you name different colors. Whenever you call out "Brown!" have them each find a brown square to stand on.

RHYME

Open Your Eyes

Open your eyes.
Look all around.
What can you see
That is colored brown?

Elizabeth McKinnon

If You Are Wearing Brown

Sung to: "If You're Happy and You Know It"

If you are
Wearing brown,
Turn around.
If you are
Wearing brown,
Turn around.
If you are
Wearing brown,
Then please
Turn around.
If you are
Wearing brown,
Turn around.

Additional verses: If you see something brown, turn around; If you like the color brown, turn around.

Janice Bodenstedt

LANGUAGE IDEA

Look through a picture book with your children and have them name things they see that are brown.

SNACK IDEA

Serve brown foods such as dry cereal mix or peanut butter on toast.

Mud

Making Mud

Place dirt in dishpans. Ask your children if they know how to turn the dirt into mud. Let them experiment by adding water to the dirt, then stirring and observing what happens. Give the children pans and kitchen gadgets to play with in the mud that they make.

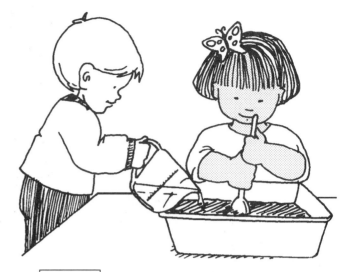

MOVEMENT

Mud Walk

Have your children pull on pretend boots. Then lead them to an imaginary puddle of thick, gooey mud. Let them walk through the pretend mud and feel it "stick" to their boots as they move their feet up and down in it.

RHYME

Mud

Mix water
With dirt,
And what
Do you think?
You'll
Have mud,
As quick as
A wink!

Jean Warren

SONG

A Hunk of Mud

Sung to: "If You're Happy and You Know It"

Oh, I wish I were
A little hunk of mud.
Oh, I wish I were
A little hunk of mud.
Then I'd ooey,
And I'd gooey
Over everybody's
Shooey.
Oh, I wish I were
A little hunk of mud!

Author Unknown

LANGUAGE IDEA

With your children, talk about making mud pies and ask them to name other things they could make with mud.

SNACK IDEA

Serve chocolate pudding "mud" for snacktime.

Pigs

HANDS-ON ART

Pink Pigs

Give each of your children a piece of white butcher paper or construction paper with a spoonful of pink finger paint in the center. Let the children use their hands and fingers to make designs on their papers. Allow the papers to dry. Then cut them into pig shapes and display them on a wall.

MOVEMENT

Pigs in the Mud

Let your children pretend to be pigs lying in a big mud puddle. Encourage them to oink and squeal as they roll around in their cool mud "bath."

RHYME

To Market, to Market

To market,
To market,
To buy
A fat pig.
Home again,
Home again,
Jiggety-jig.

To market,
To market,
To buy
A fat hog.
Home again,
Home again,
Jiggety-jog.

Traditional

Piggy's Way

Sung to: "Row, Row, Row Your Boat"

Roll, roll
In the mud,
Each and
Every day.
Merrily, merrily,
Merrily, merrily.
This is
Piggy's way!

Susan M. Paprocki

See the Little Pigs

Sung to: "Ten Little Indians"

See the little pigs
Rolling in the mud.
See the little pigs
Rolling in the mud.
See the little pigs
Rolling in the mud.
Rolling in the mud
All day.

See the little pigs
Rolling in the mud.
See the little pigs
Rolling in the mud.
See the little pigs
Rolling in the mud.
See them splash
And play.

Elizabeth McKinnon

LANGUAGE IDEA

Tell your children a pig story.
Have them oink whenever they
hear the word *pig*.

SNACK IDEA

Cut pig shapes out of large
pieces of pink construction paper
to make placemats for the snack
table. Serve a pink snack such as
strawberry yogurt.

Dirty and Clean

HANDS-ON DRAMATIC PLAY

Washing Fun

Set up a washing area that includes pans of sudsy water and pans of clear water. Let your children take turns washing and rinsing "dirty" items, such as doll clothes, doll dishes, or small toys, to make them "clean."

MOVEMENT

Bath-Time Fun

Ask your children to imagine that they are covered with dirty mud. Have them pretend to hop into the bathtub and scrub themselves clean. Let them "dry" themselves with pretend bath towels.

RHYME

Give It a Wash

Here is
A dish,
The dirtiest
I've seen.
Let's give it
A wash
And make it
All clean.

Repeat, each time substituting a different word for *dish*.

Elizabeth McKinnon

Let's Make It Clean

Sung to: "London Bridge"

This is such
A dirty shirt,
Dirty shirt,
Dirty shirt.
This is such
A dirty shirt—
Dirty shirt!

Wash the shirt
And make it clean,
Make it clean,
Make it clean.
Wash the shirt
And make it clean—
Clean, clean shirt!

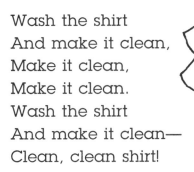

Repeat, each time letting your children
help substitute a different word for *shirt*.

Elizabeth McKinnon

LANGUAGE IDEA

Set out clean and dirty items.
Have your children name the
items and tell whether they are
dirty or clean.

SNACK IDEA

Let your children help wash fruits
or vegetables to eat for a snack.

Washing Hands

HANDS-ON ART

Hand-Print Signs

Make paint pads by placing folded paper towels in shallow containers and pouring on small amounts of tempera paint. Let your children press their hands on the paint pads, then on pieces of construction paper to make prints. When the papers have dried, let the children help display them as reminders for washing hands.

MOVEMENT

Hand-Washing Fun

With your children, pretend to turn on a giant water faucet. Let them "wash" their hands in the water with imaginary bars of soap. End the activity by pretending to turn off the faucet.

RHYME

Wash Your Hands

Be sure to wash
Both your hands
With a lot of soap.
    (Pretend to wash hands.)
Don't give cold
Or flu germs
Any kind of hope!

Susan M. Paprocki

SONG

This Is the Way

Sung to: "The Mulberry Bush"

This is the way
We wash our hands,
Wash our hands,
Wash our hands.
This is the way
We wash our hands,
So early
In the morning.

Additional verses: This is the way we
rinse our hands; This is the way we dry
our hands.

Adapted Traditional

LANGUAGE IDEA

With your children, talk about
what to do first, second, and
so on when washing and dry-
ing hands.

SNACK IDEA

Provide your children with a
special bar of soap to use for
washing their hands before
snacktime.

Farm Animals

Barnyard Mural

Cut a large barn shape and a fence shape out of construction paper. Glue the shapes on a piece of butcher paper. Give your children cutout pictures or construction-paper shapes of farm animals. Help the children glue or tape the pictures to the butcher paper to make a Barnyard Mural.

MOVEMENT

Farm Animal Moves

Lead your children around a pretend barnyard, moving like different farm animals. For example, gallop like horses, frolic like lambs, strut like chickens, or waddle like ducks. End the activity by having the children lie down like cows and "chew their cud."

RHYME

On the Farm

Theresa went
Out walking
On the farm
One day.
She met a
Little chicken,
So she stopped
A while to play.

Recite the rhyme for each of your children, substituting the child's name for *Theresa* and a different farm animal name for *chicken*.

Elizabeth McKinnon

In the Barnyard

Sung to: "The Paw-Paw Patch"

Gallop, gallop,
Little horse.
Gallop, gallop,
Little horse.
Gallop, gallop,
Little horse,
Way down yonder
In the big barnyard.

Continue with similar verses
about other farm animals.

Jean Warren

Tell a story about a farm, using
toy farm animals as props.

Let your children decorate pieces
of construction paper with farm
animal stickers to make placemats for the snack table.

To the Farm

Sung to: "Twinkle, Twinkle, Little Star"

Horses, donkeys,
Cows that moo,
Chickens, kittens,
Piglets, too.
Fish that swim
Down in the pond.
Ducklings quacking
All day long.
All these animals
You can see,
If you go to
The farm with me.

Beverly Qualheim

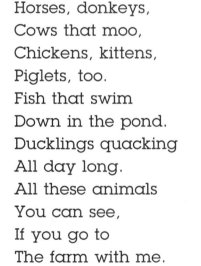

Mother and Baby Animals

HANDS-ON LEARNING GAME

Matching Mother and Baby Animals

Divide eight index cards into two sets. On one set, draw or glue pictures of different adult animals. On the other set, draw or glue pictures of matching baby animals. Give the cards to your children and let them match the baby animals with their "mothers."

MOVEMENT

Come With Mother

Pretend to be a mother horse and invite your "colts" to follow you around the room as you gallop and play. Continue by taking the roles of other mother animals such as a cat, a a hen, or a sheep.

RHYME

Playing Together

The mother sheep
Loves to play
With her baby lamb
All day.

Continue, using other combinations such as these: *mother goat, baby kid; mother cat, baby kitten; mother hen, baby chick; mother cow, baby calf; mother duck, baby duckling.*

Elizabeth McKinnon

SONG

Animal Lullaby

Sung to: "Frere Jacques"

Mother cow,
Mother cow
Sings to her calf,
Sings to her calf,
"Moo, moo, moo.
Moo, moo, moo.
Sleep, little calf,
Sleep, little calf."

Mother hen,
Mother hen
Sings to her chick,
Sings to her chick,
"Cluck, cluck, cluck.
Cluck, cluck, cluck.
Sleep, little chick,
Sleep, little chick."

Continue with similar verses about other mother and baby animals.

Elizabeth McKinnon

LANGUAGE IDEA

With your children, name mother and baby animals such as cows and calves, horses and colts, cats and kittens, dogs and puppies, and ducks and ducklings.

SNACK IDEA

When snacktime is over, pretend to be a mother animal and dismiss your "babies," one at a time, from the table.

Animal Sounds

Listen and Match

Draw or glue pictures of familiar animals on index cards. Make a tape recording of those animal sounds. Play the tape for your children. Help them identify the animal sounds and then match the sounds with the animal pictures.

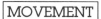
MOVEMENT

Listen and Do

Sit together with your children. Make an animal sound such as "moo," "bow-wow," or "peep, peep, peep." Have your children pretend to be that animal and act out its movements.

RHYME

In the Farmyard
In the farmyard
At the end of day,
Listen to what
The animals say.
The cow says, "Moo."
The pigeon, "Coo."
The sheep says, "Baa."
The lamb says, "Maa."
The hen, "Cluck, cluck."
"Quack," says the duck.
The dog, "Bow-wow."
The cat, "Meow."
Then the barn
Is closed up tight,
And the farmer
Says, "Goodnight."

Adapted Traditional

SONG

Old MacDonald Had a Farm

Sung to: "Old MacDonald Had a Farm"

Old MacDonald
Had a farm.
E-I-E-I-O.
And on his farm
He had a horse.
E-I-E-I-O.
With a
Neigh-neigh here.
And a
Neigh-neigh there.
Here a neigh,
There a neigh.
Everywhere
A neigh-neigh.
Old MacDonald
Had a farm.
E-I-E-I-O.

Continue with other combinations such as these: *cow, moo-moo; sheep, baa-baa; dog, bow-wow; donkey, hee-haw; turkey, gobble-gobble; hen, cluck-cluck; rooster, cock-a-doodle; pig, oink-oink.*

Traditional

LANGUAGE IDEA

Tell an animal story. Each time you name an animal, have your children make that animal's sound.

SNACK IDEA

Assign different animal sounds to different snack foods. Let your children "quack" if they want crackers, "meow" if they want milk, "oink" if they want fruit, and so on.

Barns

In the Barn

Make a barn by painting a large appliance box red. Place the box in a corner of the room. Let your children pretend to be farmers and play inside the barn with toy farm animals.

MOVEMENT

Animal Parade

Use chairs or other furniture to set up a "barn" that your children can walk through. Then let your children pretend to be different farm animals and parade around, walking in and out of the barn as they go.

RHYME

Here Is the Barn

Here is the barn,
So big, you see?
> *(Form roof with fingers.)*
In walk the cows,
One, two, three.
> *(Hold up fingers, one at a time.)*

Repeat, each time substituting the name of a different animal for *cows.*

Adapted Traditional

SONG

Out by the Red Barn

Sung to: "Down by the Station"

Out by the
Red barn,
Early in the
Morning,
See the
Little chicks
Standing in
A row.
See the busy
Farmer
Giving them
Their breakfast.
Cheep, cheep,
Cheep, cheep.
Off they go!

Continue with similar verses
about other animals such as
cows, horses, sheep, pigs,
and ducks.

Jean Warren

LANGUAGE IDEA

Place a felt barn shape on a
flannelboard. Let your children
put felt animal shapes on the
barn shape as you name each
animal.

SNACK IDEA

Glue cutout paper barn shapes
on pieces of construction paper
to make placemats for the snack
table. Let your children decorate
the mats with farm-animal
stickers.

Ducks

Feathery Ducks

Give your children duck shapes cut out of yellow construction paper. Set out yellow feathers (available at craft stores). Let the children brush glue on their duck shapes and place the feathers on top of the glue.

MOVEMENT

Mother and Baby Ducks

Take the role of a mother duck. Ask your "ducklings" to line up behind you. Then lead them around the room, waddling and quacking as you go.

RHYME

Little Ducklings

All the little ducklings
Line up in a row.
Quack, quack, quack,
And away they go.

They jump in the water
And bob up and down.
Quack, quack, quack,
They swim all around.

Elizabeth Vollrath

Little White Duck

Sung to: "Mary Had a Little Lamb"

If I were a
Little white duck,
Little white duck,
Little white duck.
If I were a
Little white duck,
This is what I'd do.

I would give a
Little quack-quack,
Little quack-quack,
Little quack-quack.
I would give a
Little quack-quack.
That is what I'd do.

Julie Israel

LANGUAGE IDEA

Float a toy duck in a tub of water and let your children make up stories about it.

SNACK IDEA

Let your children line up and waddle like little ducks to the snack table.

CHAPTER INDEX

BUSY BEES SERIES CHAPTER INDEX

Early Learning Resources

Songs, activities, themes, recipes, and tips

Celebrations

Easy, practical ideas for celebrating holidays and special days around the world. Plus ideas for making ordinary days special.

Celebrating Likes and Differences
Small World Celebrations
Special Day Celebrations
Great Big Holiday Celebrations

Theme-A-Saurus®

Classroom-tested, around-the-curriculum activities organized into imaginative units. Great for implementing child-directed programs.

Multisensory Theme-A-Saurus
Theme-A-Saurus
Theme-A-Saurus II
Toddler Theme-A-Saurus
Alphabet Theme-A-Saurus
Nursery Rhyme Theme-A-Saurus
Storytime Theme-A-Saurus

1•2•3 Series

Open-ended, age-appropriate, cooperative, and no-lose experiences for working with preschool children.

1•2•3 Art
1•2•3 Games
1•2•3 Colors
1•2•3 Puppets
1•2•3 Reading & Writing
1•2•3 Rhymes, Stories & Songs
1•2•3 Math
1•2•3 Science
1•2•3 Shapes

Snacks Series

Easy, educational recipes for healthy eating and expanded learning.

Super Snacks
Healthy Snacks
Teaching Snacks
Multicultural Snacks

Piggyback® Songs

New songs sung to the tunes of childhood favorites. No music to read! Easy for adults and children to learn. Chorded for guitar or autoharp.

Piggyback Songs
More Piggyback Songs
Piggyback Songs for Infants & Toddlers
Piggyback Songs in Praise of God
Piggyback Songs in Praise of Jesus
Holiday Piggyback Songs
Animal Piggyback Songs
Piggyback Songs for School
Piggyback Songs to Sign
Spanish Piggyback Songs
More Piggyback Songs for School

Busy Bees

These seasonal books help two- and three-year-olds discover the world around them through their senses. Each book includes fun activity and learning ideas, songs, snack ideas, and more!

Busy Bees—SPRING
Busy Bees—SUMMER
Busy Bees—FALL
Busy Bees—WINTER

101 Tips for Directors

Great ideas for managing a preschool or daycare. These hassle-free, handy hints are a great help.

Staff and Parent Self-Esteem
Parent Communication
Health and Safety
Marketing Your Center
Resources for You and Your Center
Child Development Training

101 Tips for Toddler Teachers

Designed for adults who work with toddlers.

Classroom Management
Discovery Play
Dramatic Play
Large Motor Play
Small Motor Play
Word Play

101 Tips for Preschool Teachers

Valuable, fresh ideas for adults who work with young children.

Creating Theme Environments
Encouraging Creativity
Developing Motor Skills
Developing Language Skills
Teaching Basic Concepts
Spicing Up Learning Centers

Problem Solving Safari

Designed to help children problem-solve and think for themselves. Each book includes scenarios from children's real play and possible solutions.

Problem Solving Safari—Art
Problem Solving Safari—Blocks
Problem Solving Safari—Dramatic Play
Problem Solving Safari—Manipulatives
Problem Solving Safari—Outdoors
Problem Solving Safari—Science

The Best of Totline® Series

Collections of some of the finest, most useful material published in *Totline Magazine* over the years.

The Best of Totline
The Best of Totline Parent Flyers

Early Learning Resources

Posters, puzzles, and books for parents and children

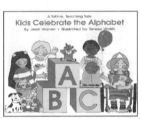

A Year of Fun

Age-specific books detailing how young children grow and change and what parents can do to lay a foundation for later learning.

Just for Babies
Just for Ones
Just for Twos
Just for Threes
Just for Fours
Just for Fives

Getting Ready for School

Fun, easy-to-follow ideas for developing essential skills that preschoolers need before they can successfully achieve higher levels of learning.

Ready to Learn Colors, Shapes, and Numbers
Ready to Write and Develop Motor Skills
Ready to Read
Ready to Communicate
Ready to Listen and Explore the Senses

Learning Everywhere

Everyday opportunities for teaching children about language, art, science, math, problem solving, self-esteem, and more!

Teaching House
Teaching Town
Teaching Trips

Beginning Fun With Art

Introduce young children to the fun of art while developing coordination skills and building self-confidence.

Craft Sticks • Crayons • Felt
Glue • Paint • Paper Shapes
Modeling Dough • Yarn
Tissue Paper • Scissors
Rubber Stamps • Stickers

Beginning Fun With Science

Make science fun with these quick, safe, easy-to-do activities that lead to discovery and spark the imagination.

Bugs & Butterflies
Plants & Flowers
Magnets
Rainbows & Colors
Sand & Shells
Water & Bubbles

Teaching Tales

Each of these children's books includes a delightful story plus related activity ideas that expand on the story's theme.

Kids Celebrate the Alphabet
Kids Celebrate Numbers

Seeds for Success™

For parents who want to plant the seeds for success in their young children

Growing Creative Kids
Growing Happy Kids
Growing Responsible Kids
Growing Thinking Kids

Learn With Piggyback® Songs

BOOKS AND TAPES
Age-appropriate songs that help children learn!

Songs & Games for Babies
Songs & Games for Toddlers
Songs & Games for Threes
Songs & Games for Fours

Learning Puzzles

Designed to challenge as children grow.

Kids Celebrate Numbers
Kids Celebrate the Alphabet
Bear Hugs 4-in-1 Puzzle Set
Busy Bees 4-in-1 Puzzle Set

Two-Sided Circle Puzzles

Double-sided, giant floor puzzles designed in a circle with cutout pieces for extra learning and fun.

Underwater Adventure
African Adventure

We Work & Play Together Posters

A colorful collection of cuddly bear posters showing adult and children bears playing and working together.

We Build Together
We Cook Together
We Play Together
We Read Together
We Sing Together
We Work Together

Bear Hugs® Health Posters

Encourage young children to develop good health habits. Additional learning activities on back!

We Brush Our Teeth
We Can Exercise
We Cover our Coughs and Sneezes
We Eat Good Food
We Get Our Rest
We Wash Our Hands

Reminder Posters

Photographic examples of children following the rules.

I cover my coughs
I listen quietly
I pick up my toys
I put my things away
I say please and thank you
I share
I use words when I am angry
I wash my hands
I wipe my nose